Unmasking
Sexual
Con Games

Parent Guide

Also from the Boys Town Press

For Parents:

Common Sense Parenting®

Getting Along with Others: Charts to Help Teach
  Social Skills to Children

Rebuilding Children's Lives: A Blueprint
  for Treatment Foster Parents

Finding Happiness in Faith, Family and Work

For Teens:

A Good Friend: How to Make One,
  How to Be One

Who's in the Mirror? Finding the Real Me

What's Right for Me? Making Good Choices
  in Relationships

One to One: Personal Listening Tapes
  for Teens

Unmasking Sexual Con Games

**For a free Boys Town Press catalog,
call 1-800-282-6657.**

**If you need help with a serious
parenting problem, call the Boys Town
National Hotline at 1-800-448-3000.**

Unmasking Sexual Con Games

Parent Guide

Ron Herron
Kathleen M. Sorensen

BOYS TOWN PRESS

Unmasking Sexual Con Games Parent Guide

Published by The Boys Town Press
Father Flanagan's Boys' Home
Boys Town, Nebraska 68010

Publisher's Cataloging in Publication
(Provided by Quality Books Inc.)

Herron, Ronald W.
     Unmasking sexual con games: parent guide/
Ron Herron, Kathleen Sorensen. – 1st ed.
     p. cm.
     ISBN: 1-889322-18-0

     1. Child sexual abuse – Prevention. 2. Acquaintance rape – Prevention. I. Kathleen Sorensen. II. Father Flanagan's Boys' Home. III. Title.

HQ57.H47 1998   649'.65
                        QBI98-116

10   9   8   7   6   5   4   3   2   1

BOYS TOWN USA
Caring for America's Girls and Boys

Dear Parent,

Recognition of the growing problem of children being born in out-of-wedlock situations has increased dramatically across the country in recent years. So much is this so that Congress enacted legislation in 1996 to provide abstinence-only education programs to promote abstinence from sexual activity until marriage.

One of the most effective ways to do so in our experience is to teach young people that they can be tricked into sexual activity by "sexual con games." If we can teach young people to unmask sexual con games, then it will be harder for them to be talked into doing something sexually that is just plain harmful.

There are many young people who are being manipulated today because they aren't as strong or aware of things as other kids are. They are being talked into sexual activity because they have been conned into believing that having sex is a way to show love.

They are the victims of people who only have their own interests at heart. They are being told that having sex is normal and something they should do so that people will love them. In truth, they are only being used.

I am recommending very highly to you the materials we have developed here at Boys Town entitled: "Unmasking Sexual Con Games." This material helps young people understand that abstinence from sexual activity outside of marriage is the expected standard for all school age children. It helps them understand that sexual activity outside of marriage is likely to have harmful psychological and physical effects. It helps them understand that bearing children out of wedlock is usually very, very harmful for the child, the child's parents and society.

This material helps young people learn how to reject sexual advances.

Thousands of young people have learned the social, psychological and health benefits of abstaining from sexual activity before marriage. This material has helped them to do so.

I very much recommend it to you. Please give us feedback on how these materials have been implemented in your own home or school.

Sincerely yours,
Val J. Peter
Boys Town Executive Director

This mask is one of many created by Boys Town students as they participate in the "Unmasking Sexual Con Games" curriculum in school. Many of our girls and boys have been victims of sexual abuse or have been involved in early sexual activity with "sexual con artists" before coming to Boys Town.

Table of Contents

Book Credits

Editing: Lori Utecht
         Lynn Holm
Production: Lisa Pelto
Page Layout: Michael Bourg
Cover Design: Brian Wilson
Mask: Boys Town Student

Introduction

Language and touch are what we first use to show our children how much we love them. We cuddle and kiss a newborn; we coo, whisper, and giggle. The child learns to return the looks, gestures, and noises in a growing awareness of the expression of love.

As our children grow, we teach them the skills they need to protect themselves. They learn to avoid the hot burner on the stove, to look before crossing the street, to walk away from a stranger offering them something. However, the dangers children face become more subtle as they grow older. Even more unsettling is the fact that some of those dangers draw on the very language and gestures of love that children have experienced in their relationships with us, their parents.

1

Language can be a powerful persuader. Your children have learned to use language to communicate with others – to express feelings or make requests to meet their needs. Unfortunately, language can also be used to manipulate and control. As an adult, you probably have learned to recognize attempts to manipulate you and have developed ways to counteract those attempts. For example, perhaps you have a ready answer for resisting emotional pressure from a friend or relative. However, it is likely that your children do not have those skills, and they need your guidance to help them recognize when someone is using language to exploit them.

Especially dangerous for adolescents are people who would manipulate them into emotional or physical relationships. When someone is tricked into a sexual encounter, that person has been the victim of a "sexual con game." The term "con game" (confidence game) is defined as a swindle in which a person is defrauded after his or her confidence has been won. Anyone who is coerced into a sexual experience has been defrauded both emotionally and physically.

Sexual con games, harassment, and even abuse are widespread and can affect youth of any age, race, or gender, attending any school, private or public. A national survey conducted by researchers at Wellesley College's Center for Research on Women, published by *Seventeen* magazine and reprinted in *USA Today*, revealed startling rates of sexual harassment in our schools. More than 4,200 female students in grades 2 through 12 completed the survey. The survey found the following true of the respondents:

♦ 39 percent were harassed at school every day during the last year.

♦ 89 percent were subjected to sexual comments or gestures.

♦ 83 percent had been touched or grabbed.

♦ When administrators or teachers were informed of the harassment, the school took action in only 55 percent of the cases.

Sadly, many teenagers have lost the innocence of childhood and the joy that comes with healthy relationships. It is our responsibility as parents to teach our teens what is acceptable behavior and what is not. Above all else, we must teach them that sexually using and abusing another person is morally and legally wrong.

This book examines the kinds of words and actions that can be used to seduce, trick, or force teenagers into a sexual relationship. Included are excerpts from actual letters written by teenagers to other teenagers, given as examples of the types of games an abuser uses to convince others to have sex. You will learn how to help your child become aware of how others may threaten or damage his or her healthy moral and sexual development. This book examines the destructive effects cultural influences can have on your children's self-esteem, leaving them vulnerable to the attentions of abusers, and will help you provide them with skills to live healthy, independent lives.

If you are a parent whose child is reading *Unmasking Sexual Con Games: Student Guide* in a class, you may notice that this book is structured in a slightly different order and includes more information. This book will give you an overall understanding of the problems facing adolescents and what you as a parent can do to protect your child. If you've picked this book up independently and would like to see some of these issues addressed at your child's school, ask your school administrators to contact Boys Town Press, 1-800-282-6657, for information about the *Unmasking Sexual Con Games* curriculum.

Helping children learn about sexual matters is sometimes a delicate issue, but when the information is presented in an appropriate and sensitive manner, it can empower them to make healthy choices. As you read this material, please remember that it is not intended to startle or scare you, but to help you protect your child. With this knowledge, you can help your child build healthy relationships and avoid the hurt and shame that result from being sexually used. We must help children learn how the sexual con artist operates and how to unmask his real intentions so that his game loses its power.

Setting
Healthy
Boundaries

Before your child can develop healthy relationships, he or she needs to understand the importance of creating a personal "safe space" in which to create and nurture new relationships. This happens by understanding and setting boundaries.

Boundaries

Boundaries are the physical and emotional distance people keep between themselves and others. Imagine a series of invisible circles around your body that determine how close you will let people get to you. These circles define your boundaries and determine how much you will share with others and how open you will be in your relationships. Physical boundaries protect your body and help you decide how and by whom you can be touched, and emotional boundaries protect your thoughts and emotions. Boundaries help you tell what's right or wrong. When someone invades your "space," that person has gone too far, and you start to feel uncomfortable.

Children begin setting boundaries at an early age. As parents, we can guide them in the process of deciding when to share personal thoughts and feelings with someone. For example, children often share their private thoughts with their best friends and family members. They allow them inside their closest emotional boundaries. Relationships with other people are not as personal. Casual acquaintances talk about "light" and non-personal topics, such as the weather, sports, and movies. Strangers may exchange only necessary information or no information at all. Boundaries change over time and with different people and situations.

Your child needs to realize that people who don't respect boundaries are not good choices for friends. Perhaps your daughter learns that a friend has shared private information about her with others. That violation of trust is also a violation of boundaries. If your son frequently gets "burned" by friends who tell personal things about him to others, maybe he has the wrong friends. Or maybe he has set the wrong boundaries and shouldn't share as much as he has been.

The following checklist will help your child assess friendship boundaries. You can go through this checklist with your child, or ask him or her to look it over privately, and then you can be available to talk about it later. If your child answers "yes" to several questions, it is time to evaluate his or her current relationships, both male and female, and teach skills that result in healthy relationships.

Boundaries Checklist

Does my friend ...

♦ Interrupt a private conversation when I am talking to someone else?

♦ Take my possessions?

♦ Tease or make fun of me?

♦ Ask very personal questions?

♦ Touch my shoulder or leg or another part of my body?

♦ Tell other people stories about me?

♦ Tell other people private information about me?

♦ Stand too close to me – making me feel uncomfortable by invading my "private space?"

♦ Say or do things in front of me that I find offensive or vulgar?

♦ Always try to sit or be next to me?

♦ Force me into doing something sexual?

♦ Physically or sexually abuse me?

Appropriate Boundaries

Your child can learn to set and maintain appropriate boundaries or help friends who may have boundary problems. The first step is to identify trustworthy peers and make friends with them. Your child probably has a pretty good idea of who among his or her peers will not reveal secrets or betray trust. Those are the kids with whom to develop friendships. Your child needs to learn to identify and avoid people who look out only for their own interests. It's much more satisfying to spend time with people who aren't always looking for something in return.

Your child needs to pay attention to feelings of comfort or discomfort – these are good indicators of right and wrong – and then learn to say "no" to peer pressure. Your child can learn how to think through and solve problems before reacting or making a hasty decision.

Suggest that your child think about times when his or her personal boundaries were violated. Who was involved? What was the situation? How can the problem be handled in the future? Encourage your child to speak up when someone or something bothers him or her. Talking to a trusted adult can be a helpful way of working through a difficult problem.

If your child finds that one person always makes him or her uncomfortable, you can suggest that maybe he or she needs to explain these feelings to the person. It's possible that the person can change the offending behavior. On the other hand, if your child's feelings go beyond discomfort to nervousness or fear, the best response for the child is to ask a trusted adult for help.

Inappropriate Boundaries

Appropriate boundaries protect a person's body, thoughts, and feelings, but when a child fails to set appropriate boundaries, a dangerous situation can result, both physical and emotional. Boundaries can be too closed – for example, never sharing personal thoughts and emotions with others – as well as too open – sharing private thoughts or physical encounters with casual acquaintances or strangers.

Signs that boundaries are too open:

♦ Saying too much about yourself too soon.

♦ Telling acquaintances or strangers your personal thoughts and experiences.

♦ Displaying affection in public.

♦ Wearing revealing clothing.

♦ Having sexual encounters with acquaintances or strangers.

♦ Being unable to say "no."

♦ Standing too close to others.

♦ Making sexual comments about other people's body parts.

♦ Trusting strangers.

♦ Believing everything you hear.

Signs that boundaries are too closed:

♦ Never sharing thoughts or feelings with anyone.

♦ Not having any friends.

♦ Not letting adults help with problems.

♦ Never asking for help, even when needed.

♦ Refusing to let trustworthy adults touch you appropriately (handshakes, hugs, pats on the back).

Relationships

Your children's relationships with their peers are an important part of their lives. These relationships, if healthy, can enrich their lives and equip them with the social skills they will need to move into adulthood. Many teens, though, get stuck in unhealthy relationships, and either don't recognize them as such, or don't know how to get out of them.

The following questions can help your children determine whether their approach to personal relationships with the opposite sex is a healthy one. You can go over the questions together, or your child may want to explore these issues privately. You might want to suggest that your child write about these questions in a journal:

- ◆ Does my friend really like me for who I am, instead of for what I can do for her/him? Explain.

- ◆ Does my friend seem too good to be true? Why?

- ◆ Is my friend putting too many demands on me? How?

- ◆ Does my friend ignore me when others are nearby? Why?

- ◆ Does my friend try to change me to what he/she wants? How?

- ◆ Does my friend do things that hurt me? What?

- ◆ Do other people tell me that my friend talks about me behind my back?

- ◆ Do I get into trouble when I do what my friend says? How?

- ◆ Do I ever feel lousy after being with my friend? Why?

♦ Have I quit doing things that I used to enjoy since I became involved with my friend? What?

Kids won't always be receptive to your efforts to help them assess their relationships: They don't want their parents to know everything that goes on in their lives. It could be embarrassing for them, or they may think you will take away whatever is good in the relationship – relationships are rarely completely negative. There is something that keeps people in abusive situations. Much of what you discuss and to what degree depends on your relationship with your child. Therefore, take your time (unless you suspect abuse). Don't push. You can give frequent reminders and ask several questions, but don't interrogate.

Moral Development

A very important responsibility that parents have in helping children build relationships is teaching moral values. This task has become increasingly difficult in today's materialistic, sex-saturated society. Parents have to prepare their kids for battles against negative influences. However, there are so many negative messages attacking our kids, zipping in from all sides, that many parents feel overwhelmed and defenseless.

The first line of defense is to develop a strong value system in your children. For them to become independent, they must receive guidance about right and wrong. Parents make a serious mistake when they don't shape values and morals in their children. Without the teaching and guidance of parents, kids lack the knowledge and experience they need to make good decisions. Poor decision-making about sexual matters usually results in harmful consequences for them.

Many parents don't hesitate to set rules for some behaviors – drinking, smoking, fighting, stealing, vandalizing, and other dangerous activities. But when it comes to sex, a number of parents are perplexed. Some absolutely forbid their children to have sex. Others feel that sexual matters are private, and they turn their eyes and ears away from what their children are doing. Fathers and mothers can have completely different views on teenage sexuality. And in many cases, sons receive different messages than daughters regarding sexual activity (i.e., it's normal for a boy and sinful for a girl).

The bottom line is this: Sex is a moral issue that has serious consequences for your children. You are your children's first and foremost teacher and role model. It is up to you to give them a strong moral foundation on which to make mature decisions.

All kids differ in their ability to grasp concepts and values. Some will be open and listen carefully to what you have to say. Others will be resistant, negative, or unapproachable. This means that you may have to vary your own behavior in order to meet your child's needs. Don't hesitate to try a new approach if you encounter negative reactions at first. If you have avoided discussing sexual matters before, a sudden openness about sex will shock your kids. Take your time, and the lines of communication will eventually open.

One other point about the uniqueness of kids: Some will act as though they aren't interested in what you have to say – "Heard it all in school, Mom." Others will seem disgusted that you would talk about such things. Some may react as though you are infringing on their privacy. Don't let their immediate reactions stop you from delivering your message. It's an age-old trick of teenagers to avoid letting their parents know what they're thinking. (You probably did it yourself.) But give them some credit. They are thinking, and they are listening. Some just need the time to let what you say "sink in." A short time after listening to you, they might be repeating your words to a friend.

For every example you provide, your kids will have a counter example. Therefore, it's important to stick to clear rules and principles, not isolated examples or exceptions to the rule. Most kids don't have the experience or maturity to act morally with just a vague concept to follow. They need specific rules regarding right and wrong.

For example, here are some reasons to give your kids for not having sex:

♦ Save yourself for your wife or husband

♦ Give yourself a better chance to develop physically and emotionally

♦ Avoid getting a negative reputation

♦ Get to know a person for who and what he or she really is, and not just through a simple physical attraction

20

♦ Be free of worries, shame, or guilt

♦ Concentrate on becoming a "whole" person instead of focusing on sexual attractiveness

♦ Avoid pregnancy, sexually transmitted diseases, and the anxiety that results from sexual activity

On the other hand, there are contrary pressures that kids will be under from the media, acquaintances, or others. These are not good reasons to have sex:

♦ "Everybody is doing it"

♦ To keep a boyfriend or girlfriend

♦ To make parents worry or to get back at them

♦ To feel grown up

♦ To express affection

♦ To satisfy curiosity

♦ To be popular

Kids need to understand that they must rely on conscience: They must be able to judge right and wrong. This takes open communication with you. Encourage it.

You will have to teach your kids how to solve problems morally as well as logically and rationally. If kids have a strong belief in their values, it won't take them long to distinguish good from bad. If their value system is weak, it will take longer. But they have to acquire that moral base now if they are to carry it into adulthood. You will have to teach them how to stop, think, and choose. They will have to take responsibility for their actions.

This book contains helpful information about how kids can avoid sexual con games and the pain that comes from being used. If kids have a strong moral foundation in the face of pressure and temptation, they will have a greater understanding of what you want to teach them.

Unmasking
the Con

You've had a chance to look at healthy boundaries as well as boundaries that can cause problems in relationships. If boundaries are not healthy, your child can become vulnerable to someone who may take advantage of, or even abuse, him or her. It's important to know about the kind of person to whom your child is vulnerable. In order to help your child, you need to know the characteristics of the manipulator.

Emotional Grooming

Manipulating someone's emotions to gain control of that person is called "emotional grooming." To groom means to prepare. The emotional groomer uses words and feelings to trick, con, or coax others into doing something wrong. Other names for an emotional groomer are player and perpetrator. "Perpetrate" means to be responsible for carrying out a crime. And that's exactly what sexually using and abusing someone is – a crime.

Emotional groomers don't know how to create healthy relationships and usually have a warped and selfish view of what others can do for them. Most have never seen or experienced the mutual respect necessary to create a healthy male-female relationship. If a groomer successfully manipulates your child, she will end up in a sexually abusive relationship under his physical and emotional control.*

Emotional grooming can happen to someone of any age. Young people who have not developed distinct and healthy personal boundaries are especially vulnerable to a groomer's tactics. Many young people do not fully understand the psychological, emotional, and social impact of engaging in sexual activity. The emotional groomer cons them into believing that sexual activity is not only acceptable but expected. Many girls who end up in such manipulative relationships have a history

* Although an emotional groomer can be of either gender, masculine pronouns are primarily used in this book for the sake of readability.

of being "people pleasers." Others may be struggling for acceptance among their peers or are hungry for attention and looking for someone to care for and protect them. They will ignore or dismiss the physical or emotional coercion just to "have a boyfriend." They receive the message that sexual activity is the way to show love, and they believe it. The emotional groomer takes full advantage of these traits.

The emotional groomer is skilled at manipulation. He covers his tracks by leaving his victims confused, humiliated, and ashamed. By the time a victim realizes something is wrong, the groomer usually has enough control over her to get what he wants.

When we teach our children about emotional grooming, we want to make them cautious, not fearful. We need to help them realize that there are many good and trustworthy people in their lives who want what's best for them. But the reality of the world requires that we also make them aware that there are some people who are out to please only themselves. We don't want to let our children get hurt emotionally and physically by someone they trust. We need to help them strike a balance that gives them the confidence and freedom to explore new relationships, while at the same time protecting themselves from manipulation and abuse. Learning about emotional grooming tactics will help your child figure out when someone is trying to use and abuse her. That's the first step.

The following material is designed to help you as a parent understand how emotional groomers go about preparing and shaping other people's behavior in order to control them. The good news is that there are ways to avoid these controlling sexual con games. The con artist is skillful, but the more your child knows about how to recognize sexual con games, the easier it will be to unmask him and see the game for what it really is.

Portrait of a Groomer

Emotional groomers sometimes disguise their con games with normal, caring behaviors in order to mask their real intent. Every time the groomer does something for someone else, he chalks it up as something owed him. He runs a system of sexual debits and credits and expects to be paid in full.

The emotional groomer repeats words and behaviors in order to control others, with little regard for the harm that could result. The groomer is tuned in only to his own needs and desires and is confused about friendship, sex, and love. Many groomers live in families where there is little love and care. They may have been rejected by parents or loved ones; they've often been abused themselves. They may have suffered the pain of being used and decided it's time to inflict some pain on others. Many have grown up with little or no knowledge of normal emotional or physical boundaries. But regardless of why groomers do what they do, the result is they hurt someone else.

Unfortunately, our culture sends the message that manipulation and control are an accepted and expected part of male-female relationships. Much of the media portray male domination as macho and desirable. Females are depicted as sexual objects to be possessed and are taught to be sexy and to "give" themselves to someone they care about. Media portrayals often closely link sex and violence. We as parents need to counter such messages. We'll talk more about that later.

There are two key elements that the emotional groomer must have in place in order to gain control over someone else: a false sense of trust and secrecy.

Trust

The first stage of emotional grooming is developing a false sense of trust. The con artist convinces someone that he is the only person in the world who can really be trusted. He swears loyalty, devotion, and undying love. At the same time, he also tries to convince her that he is the most or only important person in her life. He may try to pull a girl away from her parents by pointing out things they do against her, or telling her why they're bad for her and how they try to tear the relationship apart.

The groomer attempts to build trust by repeatedly saying things like "our love is real," "you're the best thing that ever happened to me," "trust only me," or "I'll never leave you." The perpetrator usually does take care of his victims: He may buy them gifts or protect them from others. He skillfully connects much of what he does with the word "love." A girl is easy prey once she feels sure that the groomer is loyal and trustworthy and she is convinced of

30

his "true" feelings. Throughout this process, her loyalty is tested, and the groomer's control is strengthened. After a groomer successfully weaves this web of false trust, he gets her to take part in some form of sexual or immoral behavior. The girl is assured that having sex is not only okay but is the "right" thing to do.

In healthy relationships, trust develops gradually. The emotional groomer, however, tries to rush everything; he's in a hurry to convince his victim that she should depend on and confide in him only. He spends a lot of time telling her why others should not be trusted – parents, friends, teachers. She may begin to think of him as a protector or even savior. An unhealthy dependence is created by manipulation and deceit. Teens who are hungry for attention and affection are prime targets for the emotional groomer.

The following excerpts are from actual letters from groomers to their victims. They are included to give you an idea of the conversations that take place between teens. The letters illustrate how emotional groomers go about developing a relationship with their victims. They show the false sense of trust the groomer works to create. Offensive language has been deleted; otherwise, letters have been reproduced as they were written, including grammatical and spelling errors.

> *"...I just want to talk to you in private with no one else around so I can tell you how I really feel. I won't do anything else, I promise. You will know that I can be trusted when you get to know me better. I would never hurt you or anything like that...."*

> *"...I'll treat you right and I'm not going to do anything behind your back. You are what I live for. So without you my soul is black and my heart is empty. It might sound like I'm trying to get over on you but I'm not. I mean everything I say. It comes from the heart. I cry just about every night hoping I could be with you. You're the best girl I ever had...."*

> *"...We can't let anyone break us apart. If we get into an argument or disagreement we will work it out. People here can't be trusted. Only trust me...."*

Secrecy

The second stage of emotional grooming is developing secrecy. Groomers persuade girls to keep "our little secret" safe from others. The groomer understands that what he is doing could get him in trouble. He tells the girl that their relationship is different from anything anyone else has ever experienced, that no one else could understand.

Sometimes a groomer uses force or threats to make sure a girl won't talk. He often does not have to carry through on any threats: Looks, stares, glares, or other body language can keep her under his control. Once she is fearful of what might happen if the secret is discovered, she will do almost anything to keep it hidden. She is afraid of losing what's good about the relationship at the same time that she fears for her safety. She feels that the groomer holds all the power. She begins to believe it's better to say nothing than to risk making everything worse, and she falls deeper and deeper into secrecy. The following letter excerpts illustrate how the groomer tries to keep the relationship secret:

"...We can still be secret lovers. And no one would have to know about it and it would just be our little secret. You know how much I care about you and hope you feel the same way...."

"...I won't do you wrong. Just trust me and no one else. Don't be goin' to no one else cause they'll only do you wrong. This is just between you and me my love..."

Language Cons

If a child has weak or inappropriate boundaries or has demonstrated difficulty in developing healthy relationships, he or she can be particularly vulnerable to language cons. Language cons are the words and phrases – or "lines" – groomers use to trick and manipulate their victims. Language cons sometimes make a person feel special or desired; other times they make him or her feel guilty or threatened. The words may seem sincere, but their real purpose is to control. Language cons are used to convince others to do things they shouldn't.

Although these lines may sound obvious to adults, they can be very attractive to an unaware teenager. When kids hear things over and over, they are more likely to give in to what the groomer wants. These lines are common language cons:

"Just this once. Trust me."

"You know I wouldn't do anything to hurt you."

"This is normal. This is the way it's supposed to be."

"If you love me, prove it."

As trust develops, the groomer feels more comfortable using sexual phrases and vague references to sexual contact. The groomer may start out by using words that only hint about sex: "If I had you alone... Man, you wouldn't believe how I could make you feel."

As the emotional groomer gradually progresses through the trust and secrecy phases, the language progresses also. The next step may be using slang words when talking about sexual body parts or behavior. Many boys use graphic language in the beginning to see if a girl will respond, thinking it makes them appear sexy, macho, or sexually experienced. Finally, the sexual act itself is graphically described – the perpetrator uses explicit, graphic, and vulgar language to determine whether a girl is receptive to the grooming process. If there is no rejection, the groomer sees a green light. If she protests, he will back off a little and try some other tactic.

A girl who wants to believe that someone will love and protect her can become blinded by the attention she receives. At times, she may feel safe and cared for. Other times, she may be a little frightened and worried. Even though a girl may realize that the sexual relationship the groomer wants is wrong, she may go ahead anyway. She has been fooled into thinking that sex and love are inseparable. Aside from convincing a victim to have sex, the groomer often talks her into doing other things that may result in trouble: lying to her parents, sneaking out or running away, drinking alcohol or using drugs, stealing, or getting revenge on someone.

The more socially skilled and adept at emotional grooming the perpetrator is, the less he will rely on physical force. Most victims of emotional grooming are not aware of any deceptive aspects of the grooming relationship. They have been convinced that they are willing participants; they've even been convinced that they "caused" the relationship.

Identifying Language Cons

In the beginning of a romantic relationship, it's natural for those involved to say nice things to each other. That's different from the insincere flattery of an emotional groomer. First, the intent of the emotional groomer is different. Second, the abuser relies on control, not on mutual respect.

How can you help your child distinguish between the ordinary conversation that is a part of a developing relationship and the coercive language con? The following characteristics are evident in the language of emotional groomers and perpetrators, and set their language apart from the norm:

♦ Trying to convince the victim that having a sexual relationship is the same as being in love or is the only way to prove love.

♦ Using coercive words that threaten or intimidate the victim.

♦ Treating the victim like an object or possession.

♦ Repeating words to gain the victim's trust.

♦ Using words that control or reinforce the groomer's position as "the boss."

It can be difficult for a victim to find a way to stop the abuse. She may feel powerless, afraid, and at a loss for what to do. Some victims don't make good choices; they try to solve the problem by running away, hurting themselves, getting involved with alcohol and other drugs, or even attempting suicide. The victims who stand the best chance of getting out of the abusive situation are those who go to someone who can help: a parent, trusted adult, or older friend.

The emotional groomer will be just as manipulative getting out of the relationship as he was getting into it, often blaming his victim for everything that happened: "It was all your fault. You're nothing but a whore! If you hadn't wanted me so much, none of this would have ever happened." This type of verbal abuse adds to the guilt, shame, and hopelessness that she already feels.

Remember: Although this information is focused on a male emotional groomer and female victim, the reverse can also be true. A girl can use coercive and manipulative language and behavior to gain control of a relationship. It's just as humiliating to a male victim, and it's just as wrong.

Emotional Grooming Tactics

It is frightening to realize the many tactics an emotional groomer can use to get what he wants. However, knowledge is power, and the best way to disarm him is to teach your child his tricks. A groomer is a master at discovering a victim's weaknesses. He may draw on one or more of several strategies – jealousy and possessiveness, anger, intimidation, accusations, flattery, bribery – switching back and forth as needed to gain control. The following excerpts from letters illustrate these tactics.

Jealousy, Possessiveness

The groomer feels he owns his victim's feelings and behaviors and is resentful and jealous of anyone who gets attention from his "possession":

"...I'm telling you now and one time only, I want his stuff out of your locker. What kind of fool do I look like? I'm going out with you, but your ex-boyfriend is still in your locker. No! That is not going to happen. I want his stuff out. Today! If you're my girl his stuff has to go. If you want him it can stay. Your choice...."

He also can attempt to make a girl jealous in order to get her to prove her love:

*"Hey baby, I know you saw me with *****. And I know you don't like me hanging around with her. But if we don't get it on soon, what's a man going to do? You gotta show me how much you care...."*

Teens need to understand that ownership of another's thoughts and feelings has no part in a healthy relationship.

Insecurity

The groomer will use insecurity in two ways. First, he will act insecure and ask for constant reassurance of the victim's love and loyalty to him:

"...I guess it's no big deal. I just don't think I'm really your type or good enough for you. I'm screwing too many things up. I'm not worth it. So let me know if you want to stop our relationship, I'll try to understand. I probably deserve it anyway. The way I treat you, I'm not doing it the way I'm supposed to. I guess I was wrong. I'm sorry for treating you that way...."

A second tactic is to play on the victim's insecurities or create new insecurities:

"No one else will ever want you. I'm the only one who is ever going to want you. You'd be stupid to pass up a guy like me... I'm the man. Once I'm through with you, you'll never want anybody else."

Anger

Anger is a vehicle of control, a way to get what one wants. The groomer is frequently angry and may argue violently with the victim, often yelling, screaming, hitting, or throwing things:

"...So, he called you? What was his name? I know you at least know that. I've told you not to mess with me! People get hurt when they mess with me. Unless I find out your lying to me. If I find out you are, be ready, because I'm going off. That's why I said if you left something out, tell me now...."

Anger usually leads to the groomer wanting to "kiss and make up," and, often, to having sex to "make everything better." The victim doesn't want to lose her "boyfriend" and may be afraid that he will take his anger out on her, so she agrees; therefore, anger often leads to sexual conquest:

"Today I seen ***** when I was outside with everyone. He came up there and snatched me up then beat my ass...I fought back, I don't give a **** who he is...Then after a while, my stomach started hurting and I threw up... Later I was laying on *****'s lap and he said he was sorry and we ended up doin' the nasty."

Even the language used to describe the sexual act is violent. Some groomers describe sex with phrases such as, "I'm gonna knock your boots," "Let's hit it," "I'm gonna get me a piece of that," or "I'm gonna hump your bones." Words like "knock" or "hit" reveal the groomer's true intent – to hurt and use another person. Referring to the other person as an object – "piece of that" or "bones" – enables the groomer to distance himself from the victim and makes it easier for him to use her. These are signs of a relationship that can be physically and emotionally abusive. Look for other signs: bruises, cuts, more makeup than usual, swelling, etc. These indicate a dangerous situation and should be dealt with immediately.

Intimidation

Intimidation is another powerful way to control others. The groomer is skilled at intimidating with just a look or a word. He might threaten to hurt the girl or someone she likes. The groomer could take her favorite possession and damage or destroy it as a warning of what could happen. These scare tactics often work. The girl becomes too afraid to say "no":

"...I'm not mad at you, as long as you're not lying to me. If I find out you are lying, you and me are finished. So, if you're

*not telling me something, you better spill it
now. I don't want to have to find out later
from someone else. I can find out!!"*

Accusations

The groomer may accuse the victim of
all sorts of behaviors. He could say she was
flirting with someone else or that she was talking behind his back:

*"... just tell me or not if you did any-
thing with *****. If you want him, just go
out with him. I'll get over it. It's not like you
would really care anyway.... ***** even
came up to me and said some things about
you and him, and what you did. Don't do
this to me, even when I hear this stuff, it
hurts my feelings. I wouldn't be surprised if
you're playing on me."*

Flattery

Most emotional groomers are "smooth
talkers." They use language cons that lure a girl
into thinking she is the most important person
in his world, and that he's the best guy for her.
Of course, many kids are sincere and thoughtful, and, as friendships develop, they give

44

sincere, thoughtful compliments. But there is a distinction between compliments and flattery. Flattery is excessive, selfish, and often sexually suggestive or graphic:

> "...the world is for both you and I together and no one in between. You don't have to wonder just look into my eyes and my friendship will be right with you.... Your voice is like an angel to me and you're the reason why this boy wants to carry on. I've been living on the sweet things you've said and I don't want to hide it. You are the beautiful picture that I've got in my head and what is stopping us from being alone, I don't know. If I'm the one you love, do you trust me? If I didn't care about you, I would have chosen another girl but I really want you always.... Keep 'pretty,' 'sweet,' 'tender,' 'warm,' and compassionate always.... I love you girl...!"

> "...There's a lot of things I love about you. You're smart, you have a sweet personality and you're very pretty. You're very special to me. Just thinking about you makes me happy. I really want to be there for you. You're too sweet to be treated bad...."

Status

The groomer could be a good athlete, have a lot of money, be someone who always has access to alcohol or other drugs, or have a reputation as a tough guy. He uses his popularity and status to lure his victim into a sexual relationship and keep her there:

"...I do like you a lot even though we're not going out. . . . Would I call you when there's a lot more girls that I could be calling or would I even talk to you? I'm not too good for you at all because there's no such thing. Please believe me I do care and like you and I wouldn't be wasting my time if I didn't...."

Bribery

Giving gifts can be a normal sign of friendship or love, but an emotional groomer gives gifts purposely to charm his victim into pleasing him. The girl may think that she has to do something to "pay back" the groomer for all his attention and gifts. And she wants the attention and gifts to continue:

"...If I could do it I'd buy you every-thing you wanted. Remember that sweater at the mall. That would look so good on you baby. Someday I'll buy it or steal it if I have to. You mean the world to me and I want to show you how much. You just keep being good to me, you'll see...."

Control

The goal of all of these grooming tactics is control. The groomer wants to control not only what his victim does, but also how she thinks and feels. He needs to hold power over her any way he can. Most groomers will use all of these tactics in combination to get what they want. No matter how long it may take, the groomer finds a way to make her feel completely helpless and powerless to do anything about it:

"...If you get in trouble doing any-thing wrong and I hear about it, you will deal with me. I don't want to do anything with any other girl except you. I'm the only one who is right for you. So don't play on me, OK. You wouldn't want to see me mad. Just do what I say. If you're smart you'll listen good...."

Groomers and Victims

Why do people become groomers? There are several factors that may play a part. They may be using alcohol or other drugs. They may be influenced by what they've seen in life or on TV. They may imitate male/female role models.

Why do some girls become victims, while others seem to be immune to a groomer's ploys? They may lack self-esteem or feel societal pressures to have a boyfriend. They may have accepted cultural pressures to be "people pleasers," or, like emotional groomers, have been influenced by media role models.

It's important to understand how often alcohol and drugs are part of the grooming process. The groomer may use them as an excuse to be more aggressive and more forceful in getting what he wants. Some teenagers, boys in particular, even believe that it's okay to force sex on a girl when she is drunk or high. Drugs and alcohol impair judgment, which makes teens more likely to get involved in sexual behavior. Things that may seem harmless or fun when a person is high are shown to be real problems when he or she sobers up.

Some kids develop problems with substance abuse as they try to escape the pain in their lives, beginning a self-destructive cycle. Some get hooked by just experimenting. But even if they don't get hooked, drugs and alcohol can still be trouble. Using drugs/alcohol makes them loose enough to think having sex is okay. Later, using drugs/alcohol can be a way of masking how rotten they feel.

Your Child

Helping your children may rely on your ability to pick up on the clues they are sending about what is going on in their lives. Although we probably can never be completely objective about our children, we can learn to step back and observe and describe their behavior in a more objective manner.

Here are some behaviors that may be warning signs of a problem:

♦ Staying out late at night without informing you of their whereabouts

♦ Evidence of alcohol or other drug use: red eyes, slurred speech, impaired mobility; the smell of the substance, or obvious cover-up smell

- Frequent curfew violation
- New friends
- Abrupt, negative change in behavior; mood swings
- Falling grades
- Dropping of old friends to spend time with boyfriend or girlfriend

If you notice some of these behaviors, your child may by involved in an unhealthy relationship. The next chapter discusses some steps you can take to help protect your child from such a relationship or to help him or her escape from one.

Helping
Your Child

There is one common idea the perpetrator wants his victims to believe – that he will provide safety and security. A perpetrator will repeat this theme over and over, sometimes subtly, sometimes overtly. But you as a parent know that you are the surest provider of this safety and security for your child. Having a positive relationship with your children can help make them less vulnerable to manipulation. It also gives you a good communication foundation that you can build on to teach them the skills they need in order to avoid or escape the sexual con artist.

Building a Relationship

We'll talk later about these skills in more detail; in the meantime, here are some helpful hints for accomplishing this goal:

♦ Use a calm, pleasant voice. Kids
respond better to a parent who isn't
loud, harsh, or punishing.

♦ Take time to listen and understand.
Parents sometimes view a problem as
minor when it is a source of true pain
for a young person. If a kid is hurting
inside, it's a problem.

♦ Give lots of sincere praise and compliments. Acknowledge your children's
gifts and talents.

♦ Be polite and courteous. Thank your
children for their cooperation, their
ideas, or their help.

♦ Use examples to help your children
learn acceptable social skills. Explain
how to react or what to do in a given
situation.

♦ Give reasons why your children should
or shouldn't behave in a certain way.
Kids need to see the link between
behaviors and outcomes.

♦ Be direct and honest. Some topics –
even those that may be sensitive in
nature – are best addressed in an open,
factual manner.

♦ Set and adhere to clear rules and expectations. Don't hesitate to correct inappropriate behaviors and set reasonable limits.

♦ Use your sense of humor. Even in bad situations, laughter can have a healing effect. This can include using appropriate jokes, cartoons, or funny anecdotes to lighten an otherwise serious discussion. However, be careful never to appear sarcastic or condescending.

Teach Your Children

Talk about the nine grooming tactics with your children (see pages 39-47). Explain how to recognize them and discuss why they are harmful.

Teach them how to deal with language cons. Emotional groomers are skilled at using language to trick, manipulate, and deceive victims. But you can help your children recognize and protect themselves against language cons by teaching them to observe and describe the behavior of others. They need to pay close attention to a person's actions as well as his words. The old saying, "A picture is worth a thousand words," applies here. Your child should observe how a person treats others and listen to what he says to other friends about dating, relationships, and sex. All of these can be important indicators of a groomer's hidden intentions.

Your child needs to learn skills that will enable her to be strong enough to resist giving in to threats or coercion. She must build strong relationships with adults she can trust and go to for advice.

Make sure your child understands that victims should not feel guilty. If a teen becomes a victim, he or she should focus on doing things to get better rather than feeling ashamed. Con artists are responsible for their words and actions. There are no excuses for using another person, especially in sexual ways.

The person who uses language cons most likely will be persistent and try many different angles. Your child has to be just as persistent and not give in. Help your child learn that the groomer acts on the knowledge that something repeated often enough carries the ring of truth. But coercive language used repeatedly is still coercive language.

Your child needs good friends of the same gender who can help her hear and see what she may not want to notice about someone else. In other words, friends can help a young person unmask a sexual con artist. And if your child does become a victim, she may be more likely to confide in a friend than in an adult. That friend can then assist her in getting help.

Help Children Prepare

Sexual con artists may try all kinds of sweet talk, and they can be very persuasive. Convincing someone to have sex tops their list of priorities. Kids need help knowing how to respond to the pressure of a sexual con artist. It helps if they have a ready response available and can avoid situations where they have to "think on their feet." You can practice some possible responses with your child, so she will be able to avoid the verbal traps set by someone who wants to convince her to have sex. Here are some suggestions to get you started:

◆ You don't really want me; you want sex.

◆ I'm not ready for sex. Don't try to push me into doing it.

◆ If you really care for me, you'll understand and respect my feelings.

♦ Love is not sex; love is a commitment to make each other better.

♦ You don't own my body, and I'm certainly not renting it out.

♦ Love is a two-way street. You only want it one way: your way.

♦ I respect myself. Why can't you?

♦ I have too much to lose.

♦ What part of "no" don't you understand?

♦ I care enough about you to do what's best for both of us.

♦ It's not right. I hope you understand.

As you discuss these possible responses, you and your child can come up with some of your own that you both feel comfortable using.

What Skills to Teach

Some teens haven't learned the basic skills necessary to create healthy relationships and avoid the dangers of sexual con games. It's not too late to teach them these skills – they can provide the armor your children need not only to survive, but to thrive. At the same time, you can work to create an environment that provides them with safety, stability, clear rules and expectations, and room to explore.

Following is a list of skills you could teach your child that would help him or her develop healthy relationships:

♦ Saying "no" assertively

♦ Making new friends

♦ Dealing with being left out

♦ Resisting peer pressure

♦ Controlling emotions

♦ Choosing appropriate clothing

♦ Coping with anger from others

♦ Identifying one's feelings

♦ Expressing affection appropriately

♦ Using appropriate language

♦ Clarifying values and beliefs

♦ Making moral decisions

♦ Setting goals

The final chapter in this book shows how these and other skills can be broken down into a series of steps that can then be taught to and practiced by children.

Assertiveness

Teach kids assertiveness – how to get their ideas and feelings across in a positive, forceful manner. If they are in a situation that can be harmful to them, they have to learn how to get themselves out safely. Teach your child how to say "no" when she feels that someone is trying to manipulate her or convince her to have sex. Give her words to say when she feels someone is violating her boundaries. Help her role-play different situations, acting out a common scenario or an actual incident when someone tried to take advantage of her. Discuss how she can deal with the problem, and then praise her efforts for becoming a stronger person.

Assessing Relationships

Don't assume that your children know the fundamentals of healthy relationships. Teach them the language and actions of respect, beginning with the basics: "Here's how you ask someone to a dance..." "Here's how you treat someone when you are on a date...." Explain that paying for a date isn't a green light for sex, although some guys feel that way. Dating should be based on friendship, not the expectation of sexual gratuity.

In your relationships, be sure that you are a good role model for your children. Help them examine their friendships. Help them question specific relationships and examine which are best for them and which may need to be ended. Here are some questions for your children to think about:

♦ A relationship is not healthy if one person uses the other. It should be equal. Who is giving and who is taking in this relationship?

♦ Relationships are just one portion of life. Putting too much emphasis on a particular relationship takes away from all the other aspects in your life. Has this ever happened to you? When?

♦ Relationships are always changing; some will change for the better, some for the worse. What are some ways your relationships have changed?

♦ Healthy relationships should make a person feel safe and comfortable. If you do not feel this way, why not?

♦ Look at your past relationships, both good and bad, and then describe what each relationship is like now. If it has changed, what happened to change it?

♦ Identify things that you have done or changed just to please another person. Did the other person also change?

♦ Look at present relationships. List why certain people are better friends than others.

♦ What happens when someone of the opposite sex is attracted to you? What behaviors are appropriate for a first date?

♦ Do you rush into poorly considered relationships? Are you impulsive, or do you think things out?

♦ List the qualities that you think make a good friend.

Building Friendships

Learning how to be a friend can be one of the healthiest steps a teen can take. If you can help your teen learn that all rich and lasting relationships begin as friendships, you've got a great start on guiding them into healthy relationships. A romantic relationship should come after a solid foundation of friendship has been built. Teach kids what true friends are and how they should behave and that friendship is a "two-way street." The knowledge of a healthy friendship will help your children assess all their other relationships.

Help your children learn to deal with peer pressure. Teach them to think about what others want them to do and why. Teach them to decide for themselves whether something is right or wrong, helpful or harmful, and how to get out of negative situations. Maybe the decision isn't always "yes" or "no;" possibly it is "maybe later," or "I'll wait and see."

Creating a Healthy Environment

We as parents sometimes have trouble accepting all of the duties and responsibilities that come with parenthood. Some of those duties aren't pleasant; sometimes you're going to do and say some things that your kids may not like but you know are right. Your children actually need and want you to carry out that role. They may act as if they would like free rein, but they actually feel more secure if they have structure and guidelines.

Setting Rules and Consequences

When setting up a structure in your home, make your rules and expectations clear, and review the rationales or reasons behind them. Discuss the consequences if the rules are broken, and then stick to the rules you have set. Be clear, fair, and consistent.

Let your children know what is acceptable and unacceptable. Parents too often give in when their kids say, "But everyone does it." If you don't like it and think it is wrong, then stick to your beliefs. It's okay to expect a certain type of behavior and dress from your child. Monitor your children's activities; have a "healthy paranoia." Be aware of what your children watch on TV, which movies they go to, what types of music they listen to. And if you don't approve, don't allow it in your home, or restrict and monitor the times it can be watched or listened to.

Your child should keep you informed as to his or her whereabouts, abide by curfews, and report in upon arrival home. You should know your child's friends. One way to know the company your children keep is to welcome their friends into your home.

64

You may not approve of all your children's tastes and choices, but you need to respect their right to develop their own likes and dislikes. It can be a balancing act. Some parents let their kids do whatever they want; others clamp down so heavily that their children don't get to develop their own personalities. The key is having an awareness of what's going on in your child's life. Then you can step in when you think something could go wrong.

Lines of Communication

You are more apt to be an influence in your children's lives if you work to create a warm, open relationship with them. It doesn't happen overnight, but you can create an atmosphere in which your child feels comfortable confiding in you, sharing both joys and concerns.

Work to improve communication in your home. Spend time together as a family – all of you. Create a time that is your family's, and then work to keep outside distractions to a minimum. Perhaps you can designate one night a week as family night: You could build the evening around a meal that you prepare together, or go out to dinner together. If your family tends to go separate ways in the evening, try to spend some time together. Turn off the TV, computer, and stereo, and give each other your full attention. Or build your evening around watching a favorite TV show, playing a game on the computer, or listening to music everyone enjoys. If evening schedules are too difficult to coordinate, try the weekend. Many families eat Sunday dinner together.

If your children resist conversation about their lives, try to make the setting relaxed. Maybe you could work on a project together, such as baking cookies, raking leaves, or running errands. What's awkward about "let's sit and talk about you," becomes a natural conversation over a shared task.

Family traditions are important. Perhaps you used to read to your children before bedtime when they were small, but now that they are older, you no longer have that time together. Just 15 minutes of conversation at the end of the day goes a long way toward keeping the family connected. Kids are never too old for some time and attention. You could have a weekly family meeting that allows everyone an opportunity to share what's going on in his or her life, and gives all family members the chance to participate in decision making.

Plan outings together. You should avoid a passive outing, such as going to a movie, in favor of an activity that draws you into communication with each other. These activities don't have to be elaborate or expensive. You could go on a picnic, on a hike, or even camping. You could play miniature golf, or attend a school function as a family. Your kids may groan at first, but they will soon learn to love the attention they get.

As a family, give some of your time in service to your community. Sing together in a community choir; volunteer at a food pantry or soup kitchen; lick envelopes for a political or charitable fundraising campaign. Adopt a family in need of some of the resources you can share: Perhaps the single dad down the street could use some help with babysitting; maybe a homebound elderly person would appreciate a visit or help with outdoor work. Giving to others will strengthen your family ties.

Issues of Sexuality

No matter how pressed for time you are, it's essential to spend time communicating with your kids. Be open to talking about sexual feelings and behaviors. Sexuality is confusing and sometimes frightening to them. They will be reassured to know that they can discuss their most private fears with you. Talk about the wide-ranging effects of having sexual contact – physical, moral, spiritual, legal, and social. Teach them how to respond to others' advances, and how to report inappropriate behavior.

Many adults, especially parents, find it difficult to talk openly with teens about sex. However, sex education gives youth valuable knowledge that will help them learn how to make healthy decisions regarding future sexual behavior and prevent them from making disastrous mistakes. If you are uncomfortable, you need to overcome your reluctance. Talk with a counselor or professional. Read books on sexuality, or watch videotapes on ways to teach or relate to youth about sexual issues. The essence of your teaching is that sex is a natural topic for discussion and should be discussed before your children find out about it through their own experimentation. Your kids are bombarded by media images of their culture's sexual value system. Their first opinions should be shaped by your values, not the media's.

Expressing Feelings

Your kids need to hear from you that you love them. They may groan or shrug you off when you try to show your affection, but they do want to hear it. It's when they are most unlovable that they need to hear they are loved.

Help your children learn how to put their feelings into words. Sometimes teens just need some time to say what they are feeling to learn how to approach problems and create solutions. Encourage them to draw, keep a personal journal, or write poetry. All of these things can teach them constructive ways to handle and channel their emotions.

Relationships with Other Adults

Teens, especially girls, are less vulnerable if they have a good relationship with an adult. If your child doesn't have a particularly open relationship with you, encourage her to find another trustworthy adult with whom she can be open. Adolescence is a tough time. When kids share their feelings, they are on the right path to getting some help. A supportive adult can provide guidance without being judgmental.

Examining the Culture

Help your kids to evaluate their environment. They can learn to sift through the messages their culture sends and reject those that promote the wrong values. Help them look at the tactics used in advertising, the message that they need to buy something to be loved, admired, and accepted. Many kids' heroes – professional athletes and movie stars – are hawking products on television and in magazines. Advertising feeds on insecurity and will tell you that you don't look or feel good until you buy the product.

The message of advertising is also one of instant gratification: fast food, fast cars, fast cash. Kids are taught to look for the same thing in a relationship. They expect to meet someone and boom – instant sexual gratification, with no thought about what the sexual act means or any possible consequences.

The media also send disturbing messages about women. With your kids, analyze how music videos, TV programs, and movies treat women as objects, or link violence with sexuality. Look at advertising on television and in magazines, which give inaccurate portrayals of both boys and girls, and frequently include images of girls as objects. Often, only body parts are seen – ads show bodies from the shoulders down or tight jeans from the back. No faces, no feelings, no personalities – just body parts. If a boy internalizes this message, he begins to objectify girls he knows, and they no longer exist as individuals. Many times, that's how teenage boys describe girls – as objects. They may see a girl's body as analogous to the shape and size and purpose of a car. We as parents need to teach our children, both boys and girls, how destructive it is to treat people like objects. Boys need to learn how to respond with sensitivity, how to treat girls, how to respect boundaries. The media will not do this – we have to.

Problem Solving

Your children don't automatically have the skills to handle the problems they are faced with in their daily lives. Many kids are impulsive. They need to learn how to be logical and methodical when finding solutions to problems. Encourage them to ask an adult for help. Kids may view a situation as hopeless when there actually are viable solutions that you or someone else can provide. Help them learn to look at many options before reaching a decision on solving a problem.

One effective tool for problem solving for kids is the POP method. The letters stand for Problem, Options, and Plan.

Problem – Before your child can solve anything, he or she has to know exactly what the problem is. This may sound elementary, but people often rush into making a decision before they've identified the whole scope of the problem. You can help your child identify questions that will help in piecing together the whole problem, not just the obvious parts of it. Be like a newspaper reporter: Help your child ask the "who," "what," "when," and "where" of a problem. Questions like these allow your child to sort through his or her feelings and get a better picture of the whole situation.

Options – Once your child has identified the problem, help him or her think of different ways to solve it. Encourage your child to ask, "What would happen if I did this? Or this?" Most options have advantages and disadvantages – positive outcomes and negative outcomes for each. Your child needs to examine the possible consequences of each option and take into account the situation or the person with whom he or she is dealing. Help your child determine if the positives outweigh the negatives. A solution is never perfect, but one option may have more advantages than disadvantages, so it's the one to choose.

Plan – After weighing the options, a decision is made. This is your child's plan to solve the problem.

There are times, however, when no POP plan is needed. When a guy is talking lewdly, trying to coerce your daughter into having sex, or a similar situation, the answer needs no problem-solving – it's an immediate "no!"

Teach your children that they cannot change the past; rather, they should concentrate on learning new skills that will help them in the future. They need to learn how to set and reach goals. Being forward-focused keeps past mistakes from looming too large.

Sexual Abuse

Sexual abuse is an extremely complicated problem. Many studies indicate that a lack of adequate knowledge and appropriate sexual information on the part of both youth and adults compounds the problem. All youth need sufficient information and education about values and a positive attitude that allows them to identify and avoid sexual abuse.

Signs of Abuse

In spite of parents' best efforts to protect their child, abuse can happen. The abuser is often someone within or close to the family – a step or biological parent, sibling, relative, neighbor, friend. Parents should be aware of the signs of sexual abuse and have an understanding of its impact. For children who have been abused, healing is possible only with the help of educated, caring adults. Remember: Many times youth have been taught to keep their abuse a secret.

The following behaviors may be indications of sexual abuse:

Wrestling and tickling – These can be normal childhood behaviors, but they also can take on sexual overtones. Wrestling and tickling can be painful or humiliating to the person on the receiving end. Wrestling, tickling, or roughhousing can be sexually stimulating and can lead to more explicit sexual activities.

Obscene language – Youth, especially young children, who refer to adult sexual activities in explicit ways may be doing so because this language was used toward and against them while they were being sexually abused.

Frequent touching – Although touching may seem harmless, it may lead to more intimate behavior. Touching can be a subtle form of foreplay. A youth who frequently touches adults may have learned this from an abuser.

Self-mutilation – Tattoos, cigarette burns, hickeys, cuts on the arms and legs, can be signs of the loss of self-respect and the powerlessness kids feel regarding what happens to them.

Combination of violence and sexuality in artwork or schoolwork – Youth express themselves in words, art, and play. Pay attention to subtle signs.

Overt sexual acting out toward adults – Many sexually abused youth associate sexual behavior with adult acceptance and caring.

Extreme fear or revulsion when touched by an adult of either sex – Touching often has been foreplay for them, or has eventually led to a sexually abusive situation. Being touched affectionately by an adult may not be viewed as pleasurable by the youth; it may be viewed as threatening or terrifying.

Running away – Kids either run away from something or to something. They may be running away from a sexually abusive environment or to a place they think is safe. Many times, running away will result in sexual or drug-oriented behavior.

Signs of distress in the child – Depression, feelings of guilt, learning difficulties, changes in normal behavior, hysterical seizures, phobias, nightmares, compulsive rituals, self-destructive or suicidal behavior.

Helping Your Child Get Better

Abuse wounds everyone in the family. Once you become aware of the problem, you need to help your child heal and get help for yourself so you all can put your lives back together.

Talk to a counselor, teacher, minister, or other trusted adult. If you don't know where to turn for professional help, call the toll-free Boys Town National Hotline at 1-800-448-3000. Counselors are on call day and night.

Help your child understand that change is possible. What happened was not your child's fault; someone took advantage of him or her. It's time to begin a new life free from abuse.

Encourage your child to admit that something terrible happened. He or she should not make excuses for the abuser or hide the secret anymore. The pain will never stop if your child doesn't do something to end it so healing can begin.

Help your child learn to recognize people and situations that can get him or her into trouble. Do some problem-solving to find ways to avoid or get away from these negative influences. Identify the situation, think of ways to handle it, and then pick the best option.

Your child may be fearful or anxious. Help him or her to recognize those feelings; expect strong emotions. Together, read some books on overcoming negative feelings and put them to work for you. If your child is depressed, ask for help; if you're angry, learn to channel that energy to a constructive activity. Together, get involved in positive activities. Join a support group. Exercise. Doing kind and helpful things for others will help you avoid getting bogged down in self-pity.

Treatment

More than anything, a child who has been sexually abused needs consistent love and support. Some children, however, may need additional help such as that provided by specially trained therapists. Therapy can provide your child with opportunities to express and clarify thoughts and to work through painful feelings. Several types of treatment are available to you and your child.

♦ Individual therapy usually occurs on an outpatient basis with a clinical social worker, clinical psychologist, or psychiatrist.

♦ Group therapy is especially helpful with teenage victims. Treatment gives them a chance to overcome some of their feelings of isolation ("No one has ever experienced anything like I did") and to eliminate the secrecy associated with sexual abuse. In a group, they have the chance to receive support for their feelings and rights and see that others have learned to act upon these feelings in a positive way. They also learn interpersonal skills that help make them less vulnerable to being victimized again.

♦ Inpatient treatment is sometimes required for youth who are at great risk for self-destructive behavior. Hospitalization can provide the safety and medical supervision required for those who are temporarily over-whelmed by feelings associated with their abuse and possible mental illness.

Most sexually abused youth need a chance to resolve complex issues that are associated with their victimization. Your child may be dealing with one or more of these issues:

Believability. Your child may have tried to speak to you or someone else about the abuse but felt that he or she wasn't believed. The child needs repeated assurance that you do believe it and that disclosing the abuse was the right thing to do.

Guilt and Responsibility. Frequently, the abuser will blame the youth for the abuse, saying the youth was seductive and "asked for it." The youth also may be blamed by other family members for breaking up the family or for bringing shame upon the family. The child needs to be reassured regularly that he or she is not responsible for the abuse. The victim must know that all aspects of the abuse were the abuser's fault.

Body Image and Physical Safety. Sexually abused youth need to discuss how they feel about their bodies. Many think that their bodies caused the abuse and punish themselves accordingly. They also may need to realize that as a consequence of their abuse, they use their bodies to gain inappropriate attention and rewards. They need to be taught how to respect and care for their bodies. Such supportive learning helps combat the "damaged goods" feeling of being a sexual abuse victim.

Secrecy and Sharing. By discussing what behaviors and thoughts can be shared or can be kept private, your child learns that relationships can be chosen, instead of forced upon her or him.

Anger. Your child needs to explore her or his angry feelings about the abuser. During this process of exploration, children can learn new and appropriate skills to recognize and express anger.

Powerlessness. Your child needs to learn how to regain a sense of control of her or his own life, rather than being controlled by abusers and others. On the other hand, he or she needs to learn appropriate limits, so as to not overdo it and try to control everything.

Shame. Sexually abused youth often are left feeling contaminated, as if there is something fundamentally wrong with them. The worst thing that can happen to them, they may believe, is for someone else to see or know their basic flaw. If your child has been sexually abused, he or she must own and work through such feelings of shame. This is possible with your understanding and love.

Your attitude in dealing with your child's abuse will have a great impact on how your child responds to treatment. Be honest, and share information. Unfortunately, some parents think that they will unduly upset their children by allowing them to know that terrible things such as sexual abuse occur. They think that it is much better to shelter their children from this reality. Similarly, children may not want to disclose information regarding abuse because they think their parents will not believe them. As they see their parents avoid the topic, they too learn to hide or avoid talking about it. A cycle of avoidance is developed, and the secret of sexual abuse continues. It is much healthier to give your children as much information as you can about the tragedies of sexual abuse.

Striking a Balance

Be open about discussions of both sexual abuse and positive relationships. Negative descriptions of people or relationships need to be balanced with positive descriptions of people or relationships. In other words, your children need not be fearful that everyone is an abuser; they need to know that there also are many caring people with whom they can build healthy relationships. If your children learn both the "good" and "bad," they form a much better perspective on sexuality and will be less likely to be alarmed by any discussion of sexual abuse.

Teach your children the difference between "good" secrets and "bad" secrets. This may take a great deal of time because it involves learning to identify emotions and feelings. In other words, teach about the emotional burden that comes with a bad secret and the good feeling that goes with knowing a good secret that later will be shared with others. For example, a bad secret is when a child is frightened or conned into never telling anyone that she and "Uncle" have a "special" sexual relationship. A good secret is when a child knows there is a surprise birthday party planned for one of her friends. There is an enormous difference regarding the impact these two secrets have on a child's life, and yet the child may not be able to distinguish between them. If your child starts displaying behaviors that signal withdrawal into secret relationships, some type of abusive relationship may be indicated.

Speak to your child in an even, matter-of-fact voice. One of the primary skills you should develop is the ability to handle sexual discussions in a way that promotes openness and seriousness. This also means that you should talk to your children using anatomically correct language, providing them with proper

83

sexual terms. Above all, believe what your children tell you, and tell them you are going to trust them.

Working for Change

It is possible to change the sexual attitudes and behavior of young people and protect our children from the sexual con artist. It all starts with education. We as parents cannot prevent our children from ever seeing another harmful TV program or interacting with people who might hurt them. What we can do is give them enough information to make good choices on their own. They have to be media literate and have the skills to reflect on the messages being sent. They have to have the ability to recognize when another person is trying to manipulate them. They also have to learn how to create healthy boundaries and positive relationships. Some people are going to try to cross those boundaries. Kids have to have enough information, education, and positive relationships with adults to avoid being used.

We as parents need to instill solid moral principles in our children. We must continue to fight against the negative images that influence their ideas about what it means to be a man or a woman – about how to love and how to be in a relationship. Most important, we must provide them with the love, respect, and role-modeling they need to become productive, moral citizens.

Teaching
Skills

As human beings, we live in social groups. We learn early in life that there are consequences, both positive and negative, attached to how we interact with others and how we choose to respond in social situations. This process of "socialization," which begins in the earliest interactions between infant and parent, prepares us for more complex situations. Ideally, lessons learned at each stage in our development become the tools that we use to meet the demands of later stages of life.

Today, however, kids face many more challenges as they work to interact with others in socially acceptable ways. When your kids use social skills appropriately, it increases the likelihood that they will know what to do or say when they deal with other people. That in turn means they are more likely to be successful in their relationships. You also can teach them how, why, and where they should use these skills. Parents who teach social skills to their children are equipping them with "survival skills" for getting along with others, for learning self-control, for building healthy relationships, and for protecting themselves from abusive relationships.

The focus of this chapter is on the development of these abilities in your children. Activities that many people find quite easy, such as making new friends or expressing affection appropriately, can present major hurdles for a young person who has not developed effective social behaviors. In addition, a child who is capable of using appropriate social skills still may have difficulty recognizing when, where, and with whom to use a particular skill.

Your child also needs to learn how to "read" other people's social behaviors and cues. Successful social interactions depend largely on the ability to understand the nonverbal behaviors of others and to show sensitivity to their feelings and points of view.

When teaching social skills to youth, you need to break the skills into smaller parts that your children can master. At first, your child may have difficulty connecting these separate parts into one smooth skill, so be patient. As parents, we should spend time teaching important skills to our kids before they need to use them. When children know what is expected of them and have the opportunity to prepare, they are more successful.

Proactive Teaching

Proactive Teaching is teaching that is done at a neutral time in order to prepare kids for future situations. In other words it is "preventive" teaching because it helps kids learn what they need to know before they ever have to use it.

You have probably used this type of "preventive" teaching already, especially when your kids were young – teaching them how to cross the street safely or how to telephone for help. Proactive Teaching is a simple concept, but most parents do not use it as often as they could, and they tend to use it less often as kids grow older. There are two types of situations in which you can use Proactive Teaching:

♦ When your child is learning something new.

♦ When your child has had difficulty in the past with a certain situation.

Here are some examples of situations in which other parents have used Proactive Teaching. Before the occasion arose, they taught their children to:

♦ Apologize for getting in a fight.

♦ Say "No" if someone offers them alcohol.

♦ Accept a "No" answer.

♦ Answer a police officer's questions.

The possibilities for using Proactive Teaching are endless, and they can and should be adapted to your own family.

The steps of Proactive Teaching combine clear messages and kid-related reasons with practice. Practice gives your children an opportunity to see how they would use the skill before they are in the actual situation. Here are the steps of Proactive Teaching:

Describe what you would like – Be specific, and make sure your children understand: "Sharon, when your teacher criticizes you for something you have done in school, you need to look at her, listen to what she says, say you understand, and then work to change whatever behavior she has asked you to change."

Give a reason – What if your 16-year-old thinks the idea of developing a better response to her teacher – or better social skills, for that matter – is pointless? Many children do not understand the relationship between their behaviors and consequences. That is where rationales come in. Rationales are fundamental reasons for doing things. We use them every day to convince ourselves or others of the benefits or drawbacks of maintaining or changing a behavior. For example, a rationale for showing sensitivity to others is that if you help and encourage others, they are more likely to help and encourage you. A rationale for being on time for work is that your boss may take that into consideration when deciding whether to give you a raise. Anytime you can help your child to discover a personally valid rationale for a given behavior, you are likely to have his or her cooperation.

Children, like adults, benefit from knowing why they should act a certain way: "When you show respect to your teacher, she will be more likely to respect you and listen to what you have to say."

Practice – Younger children like to pretend and play different roles in the practices. Working with older children and adolescents can pose more of a challenge. Set up the practice with the idea that you're going to explore better ways of handling a situation: "Okay, Sharon, let's say your teacher has just told you she's unhappy with the fact that you've been late to class twice this week. Show me what you would say and do to respond appropriately."

After using Proactive Teaching several times to teach a skill, you may only need to provide a reminder – a preventive prompt – when your child is going to be in a situation where he or she needs to use the skill. Let's say that you have practiced with your daughter on how to respond to her teacher. Before she goes to school, you could say, "Remember Sharon, if you receive criticism in class, stay calm, like we practiced. Look at your teacher, listen to what she says, and then say you understand." The purpose of a preventive prompt is to get your child focused on what you have practiced.

Proactive Teaching can promote gradual behavior changes in problem areas and can help prepare children for unfamiliar situations. It can increase your children's self-confidence by showing them that they can learn how to change their behavior. Perhaps most importantly, Proactive Teaching allows you and your children to work toward goals together. Taking the time to be with your children and showing them that you care helps improve your relationship with them, and helps them build healthy relationships with others.

It is important for your kids to understand that social skills are lifelong survival skills, not devices that allow you to control them, as they may think. Personalize the skills as much as possible, your kids will be able to see the relevance of the skills to their own lives: "It won't be long before you are out on your own"; "When you go to college next year"; "When your boyfriend asks you to...." Tie new skills into skills your kids have learned in the past: "Do you remember last year when you were in trouble with the principal and you...." You also might want to discuss anecdotes from your own life, both your successes and failures. As you see your children attempting new skills, give them plenty of praise and perhaps other rewards. The process may be slow, but don't wait for perfection; praise their successes, even with using small steps of the new skills. It won't be long before you notice improvements in their relationship with you and with others.

As part of a system of reinforcement, you also need to give negative consequences when your child fails to respond appropriately. If your kids haven't received consequences from you in the past, they are likely to be somewhat confused and resistant. Remain firm and consistent; they'll eventually see that you are serious, and you will begin to see results.

Start small. Choose one or two skills, rather than bombarding them with too much new information. Again, progress may be slow, but don't be deterred; they will eventually come along if you are consistent and patient.

Following are some examples of social skills that build healthy relationships you might teach your children. They have been broken down into manageable steps to make it easier for your child to master them. The first skill includes an example of rationales you might give your child for each step, and helpful hints to help him or her learn the new skill.

Disagreeing Appropriately

Some people might think that if two people disagree, they have to argue or fight. That's not true. By learning how to disagree appropriately, you can avoid arguments and unpleasant situations that can arise when people don't see eye to eye. It's important to express your opinion when you disagree. Following these steps allows you to do that calmly and clearly. Your opinion will be taken more seriously when you use this valuable skill.

Step 1. Look at the person.

Rationale: Looking at the person shows that you are paying attention.

Helpful hints:

♦ Don't stare or make faces.

♦ Keep looking at the person throughout your conversation.

♦ Be pleasant, and smile.

♦ Look at the person as you would a friend.

Step 2. Use a pleasant voice.

Rationale: The person is more likely to listen to you if you use a pleasant voice.

Helpful hints:

- ♦ Speak slowly and clearly. Don't mumble.

- ♦ Use short sentences. They are easily understood.

- ♦ Keep a comfortable distance between you and the other person while you are talking.

- ♦ Smile. People are more comfortable talking with someone who is friendly.

Step 3. Say, "I understand how you feel."

Rationale: Saying you understand gets the conversation off to a positive start.

Helpful hints:

- ♦ Plan ahead of time what you are going to say.

- ♦ If you still feel uneasy about how you are going to start your conversation, practice.

- ♦ Start to discuss your concerns as part of a conversation, not a confrontation.

- ♦ Be sincere.

Step 4. Tell why you feel differently, using specific descriptions.

Rationale: Using vague words can lead to confusion and doesn't get your point across.

Helpful hints:

♦ Use as much detailed information as possible.

♦ Be prepared to back up what you say.

♦ If necessary, practice what you are going to say.

♦ Always remember to think before you speak.

Step 5. Give a reason.

Rationale: Your disagreement will carry more weight if you give a valid reason.

Helpful hints:

♦ Be sure that your reasons make sense.

♦ Support your reasons with facts and details.

♦ One or two reasons are usually enough.

♦ Remember to stay calm during the conversation.

Step 6. Listen to the other person.

Rationale: Listening shows you respect what the other person has to say.

Helpful hints:

- ♦ Don't look away or make faces while the other person is talking.
- ♦ Don't interrupt.
- ♦ Stay calm.
- ♦ Don't argue.

Use of Appropriate Language

1. Decide what thoughts you want to put into words, and then say them.

2. Look at the situation and the people around you.

3. Know the meanings of words you are about to say.

4. Refrain from using words that will be offensive to people around you or that will not be understood.

5. Avoid using slang, profanity, or words that could have a sexual meaning.

Saying "No" Assertively

1. Look at the person.
2. Use a clear, firm voice.
3. Say, "No, I don't want...."
4. Request that they leave you alone.
5. Remain calm but serious.

Coping with Anger from Others

1. Look at the person.
2. Remain calm, and breathe deeply.
3. Use a neutral voice and facial expression; no laughing or smirking.
4. Avoid critical or sarcastic comments.
5. Listen to and acknowledge what the other person is saying.
6. If the other person becomes aggressive or abusive, remove yourself from the situation.
7. Report the incident to an adult.

Dealing with Being Left Out

1. Accurately identify that you have been left out.

2. Remain calm, and monitor your own feelings and behavior.

3. Either find another positive activity to engage in, or locate an adult to talk with.

4. Possibly discuss your feelings with those who initially left you out. Remember to give and accept criticism appropriately.

Expressing Appropriate Affection

1. Identify the other person.

2. Decide on the appropriate boundary or level of closeness between you and the other person.

3. Choose the appropriate behaviors to match the situation and that level of closeness.

4. Assess the other person's comfort with the situation and your affectionate behaviors.

5. Refrain from overly physical displays of affection in public or with people you have only recently met.